Astrology For Beginners:

Zodiac Sign, Astrology Aspect and Astrological Compatibility Guide

By

Karen Brown

Table of Contents

Introduction 5

1. Aries 6

2. Taurus 9

3. Gemini 12

4. Cancer 15

5. Leo 18

6. Virgo 21

7. Libra 24

8. Scorpio 27

9. Sagittarius 30

10. Capricorn 33

11. Aquarius 36

12. Pisces 39

Final Words 42

Thank You Page 43

Astrology For Beginners: Zodiac Sign, Astrology Aspect and Astrological Compatibility Guide

By Karen Brown

© Copyright 2015 Karen Brown

Reproduction or translation of any part of this work beyond that permitted by section 107 or 108 of the 1976 United States Copyright Act without permission of the copyright owner is unlawful. Requests for permission or further information should be addressed to the author.

This publication is designed to provide accurate and authoritative information in regard to the subject matter covered. This work is sold with the understanding that the publisher is not engaged in rendering legal, accounting, or other professional services. If legal advice or other expert assistance is required, the services of a competent professional person should be sought.

First Published, 2015

Printed in the United States of America

Introduction

Astrology is a study of patterns and co-relations between celestial bodies and the living beings, here on Earth. Every celestial event or movement in the sky affects how humans behave on Earth which is tracked through Astrology. Astrology means *"Science of the Stars"*, and has been around for many years to help us understand the influence of the celestial bodies in the past, the present and the future.

There are 12 Astrological signs formed in a great circle called the *'Zodiac belt'*. These signs refer to the position of the sun when a birth takes place. The sun spins around this belt day by day, month by month, affecting and transferring celestial radiation to the Earth. Below is a complete description and characteristics of the 12 signs to help you understand yourself and others better.

1. Aries

Aries (March 21 – April 20)
Symbol – The Ram

Element – Fire
Compatibility – Leo, Sagittarius, Taurus, Gemini, Aries
Conflicting Signs – Cancer, Libra, Virgo, Capricorn
Key Traits – Born leader, headstrong, impulsive, and ambitious
Strength – Self-Confidence, determination, Energetic, go-getter
Weakness – Impatience, pushing too hard, argumentative
Ruling Planet – Mars
Keyword – I am

Aries is the first sign of the zodiac, so naturally, it represents headship. Being born as an Aries means that these people are always keen on taking initiatives in everything they do. They are fearless, dynamic, and competitive. They don't hold back and aren't afraid to explore the unknown even if it means taking risks.

They are independent, energetic, and adventurous and love to travel. They have the natural ability to lead and do it well. Aries do not like being told what to do and often opt to run their own business on their own terms.

Dreams and achieving their goals is important to Aries. People around them admire their dedication and their go-getter attitude. The one quality that makes it easy for an Aries to fulfil goals and dreams is their 'energy'. They do not let laziness get in the way and continue to follow their passion until they reach the target.

Their impulsive attitude can make them very demanding, argumentative and intolerant towards other people sometimes. Their number one priority is to get the work done without procrastination getting in the way which is good but at times they push themselves too hard, both physically and mentally which is bound to take a toll on the body.

Compatibility: This sign is most compatible with fire signs like Leo, Sagittarius, Taurus, Gemini and Aries. When it comes to love, Aries can make wonderful partners as it is a sign of fire. Generally, Aries are flirtatious in nature. They are adventurous and always take the initiative in relationships too. That being said, the right partner with the same level of energy and passion can make an Aries weak in the knees. They are very passionate and charismatic in romantic relationships however they need reassurance of their partner's love every now and again to keep loyal.

2. Taurus

Taurus (April 21 – May 21)
Symbol – The Bull

Element – Earth
Compatibility – Virgo, Cancer, Gemini, Capricorn, Pisces, Aries
Conflicting Signs – Leo, Scorpio, Libra, Aquarius, Sagittarius
Key Attributes – Sensual, dependable, secure, decisive, faithful, and stubborn
Strength – Musical, dependable, patient, practical
Weakness – Possessive, inflexible, obstinate
Ruling Planet – Venus
Keyword – I possess

The second sign of the zodiac, Taurus love comfortable and pleasing things and situations around them. Their priorities are pretty simple. They need a secure, luxurious life with a good home, food and wine.

They are cautious, patient, practical and purposeful. They are also very thoughtful and particular about things they love and take hours to make important life choices, only so they are 100% sure of their actions.

These people do not fancy the word 'No' and make a point to complete a task once they put their mind to it even if there are obstacles along the way. So, where there is an important project to completed, you can always count on a Taurus.

They are known for their apparent stubborn and at times arrogant attitude as perceived by others. Once they decide on something, they make a point to stick to it even if it's not the best decision. Often, they don't encourage other's opinions and suggestions out of pride in such situations.

Taurus' mascot being The Bull makes them strong headed and sometimes really stubborn and hot headed too. But don't get them wrong, their sole intention is to simply get things done perfectly and on time. They understand how hard they are on themselves too so they often reward themselves with expensive gifts and goodies.

Folks born under this sign are ruled by the Earth which makes them pretty cautious of their actions. They are always aiming to keep everything under control and balanced around them. Since we are talking about a bull here, fit of rage every now and then is a given. But as mentioned before they are very practical and balanced so even when they are angry, they come back to a normal, gentle state of mind on their own.

Compatibility: Bulls are most compatible with Virgo, Cancer, Gemini, Capricorn, Pisces and Aries. Romantically, Taurus-born are loyal, caring and somewhat possessive. They rely on their heart rather than their brains when it comes to love. They express love through physical touch and intimacy. They are dependable and would go the extra mi e to make their mates happy.

3. Gemini

Gemini (May 22 – June 21)
Symbol – The Twins

Element – Air
Compatibility – Cancer, Leo, Gemini, Aquarius, Libra, Aries, Taurus
Conflicting Signs – Pisces, Virgo, Sagittarius, Scorpio, Capricorn
Key Attributes – Talkative, Thinker, Social, Multi-tasking and adventurous
Strength – Inquisitiveness, Innovative, Affectionate, Kind, Flexible
Weakness – Erratic in love, Short attention span, Nervous
Ruling Planet – Mercury
Keyword – I think

Gemini is third sign of the zodiac and is ruled by Mercury. Geminis are all about putting their brains to work ALL the time. They are intelligent and love to express what they truly feel. Geminis are known to challenge themselves and attempt to do better every day. They dwell towards anything that looks challenging to stimulate their intelligence and put their mind to work as much as they can.

Geminis are easily attracted towards intellectual and witty individuals. They are great talkers and love collecting information to further share the word with other folks. These people have a unique quality of looking at both sides of a situation and that's what their mascot *'the twins'* represent.

Geminis often experience erratic mood swings. You may notice unpredictable and irregular behaviour when around them one minute and absolutely the opposite the next minute. That's a Gemini for you!

They are adaptable to situations and very cautious when dealing with people. They have one agenda at hand, *'to do everything they can'* which often takes a toll on them. Though Geminis are known for multi-tasking and can often handle many tasks successfully but sometimes the immense pressure can cause them to fall unable to get the work done a 100%.

Geminis are always looking for something new to explore and talk about it. They are fun to be around and as long as there is a Gemini in the room, nothing can be boring. Geminis defy age both physically and mentally. Even when they age, they take their fun loving nature alongside.

Compatibility: A Gemini is most compatible to Aries, Leo, Libra, Aquarius, Cancer and Gemini. Romantically, Geminis get attracted to intelligent and talkative individuals just like themselves. Their fun-loving and flirtatious and may take a while to settle down as they constantly look for people who like exploring new things and expressing their true feelings.

4. Cancer

Cancer (June 22 – July 23)
Symbol – The Crab

Element – Water
Compatibility – Pisces, Taurus, Virgo, Scorpio
Conflicting Signs – Sagittarius, Libra, Aquarius
Key Attributes – Sensual, faithful, instinctive, Over-reactive, moody, and sympathetic
Strength – Sensitivity, persistence, loving, protecting the loved ones
Weakness – Insecure, clinging to the past, manipulative, impassive
Ruling Planet – Moon
Keyword – I nurture

Cancer is the fourth sign of the zodiac and the only sign that is ruled by the Moon. Cancer being a water sign is very emotional and highly sensitive in nature. Just like water, cancer is adaptable but does thing depending on the mood just like the tides.

People born under this sign are as important as water to many close ones. Cancerians believe in following their heart and intuition and often do what they feel right. Cancerians don't encourage other's advice as far as their personal life is concerned.

They are natural home lovers and enjoy the comfort of their home and familiar faces around. Cancers are nurturing and supportive towards family and friends. Home is the happiest place for these people. They are spiritual and highly devoted towards traditions and festivals.

These folks have a photographic memory and hold every story close to their hearts. Cancers are emotional and they are okay with it too. Their mascot is crab and just like the little shelled-creature, a Cancerian protects him/herself through a hard shell. When their feelings are hurt or if it suits their needs, the Cancers quickly retrieve back to their shells to protect themselves from the outer world. This happens more than you can imagine as sometimes even tiny events or subjects can tick Cancers off compelling them to jump right into their second home – the shell. However, this is temporary; eventually crabs do come out of their shells when they feel safe.

Crabs know how to get things done and if their kind nature doesn't do it, they use emotional manipulation to get what they want. Friends and family often turn to them for compassion and advise when in need. And the reason they do that is because Cancers never turn their back on close ones and lend a helping hand whenever they can.

Cancer is ruled by the Moon, the Great mother of the heavens which naturally makes Cancers very inclined towards nurturing and taking care of the people around them. To Cancers all that matters is a comfortable and peaceful home, loving friends and family.

Compatibility: Cancerians are most compatible with other water signs including Pisces, Taurus, Virgo and Scorpio. They are tender and gentle in love and as mentioned above they are extremely nurturing and compassionate towards their partners. They are loyal, faithful and make a perfect husband/wife to a well suited lover.

5. Leo

Leo (July 24 – August 23)
Symbol – The Lion

Element – Fire
Compatibility – Leo, Sagittarius, Cancer, Libra, Aries
Conflicting Signs – Virgo, Pisces, Capricorn, Scorpio
Key Attributes – Motivated, ambitious, loyal, charitable, dignified, and striking
Strength – Humor, pride, cheerful, creative, warm nature
Weakness – Arrogance, mulish, lazy, self-centered
Ruling Planet – Sun
Keyword – I shine/ I will

Leo is the fifth sign of the zodiac and it is ruled by the Sun. People born under this sign are self-motivated, bright and ambitious. They try to make every aspect of their life perfect, be it love, social or work life.

Just like the lion, Leos are known to attract interest of other people even without trying too hard and easily become the center of attention where ever they go.

They are social animals, creative, energetic and as many may say, the life of the party. Like the lion, they are impossible to ignore or resist.

With their strong mind and powerful persona, Leos consider themselves to be the king or queen of the room/group. These natural leaders strive to achieve the best things in life and do whatever it takes to fulfil their dreams and goals.

If there is any sign that's *'generous'*, it's the Leo. They are charitable and if need be, they don't hesitate to do other's part as well. But Leos are not always warm at heart. Since this sign is associated with fire and the Lion, sometimes they can be hot-headed and arrogant. People born under this sign are strong, courageous and fearless.

These folks are enthusiastic and they have strong interest in games and sports, which includes both indoor and outdoor games. They are true hustlers and as their keyword suggests, they believe in doing things rather than just dreaming about it. Leos can be good employees as they are active and hardworking but their leadership trait makes them great bosses as they possess an optimistic attitude towards life overall.

Leos' generosity is not limited to the underprivileged; they often like to treat themselves with the fancy things in life. So as long as they have money, they believe in spending it lavishly like a king/queen.

Compatibility: Leos are most compatible with Sagittarius, Cancer, Libra, Leo and Aries. When it comes to love, Leos are loyal, loving and passionate. Love and sex is important to Leos and they look for partners of the same level and interests. They are adventurous, creative and very energetic and they love to share that with their partners.

6. Virgo

Virgo (August 24 – September 23)
Symbol – The Virgin

Element – Earth

Compatibility – Cancer, Taurus, Capricorn, Scorpio, Pisces

Conflicting Signs – Sagittarius, Aquarius, Libra, Aries

Key Attributes – Sympathetic, sensual, faithful, instinctive, moody, and charitable

Ruling Planet – Mercury

Keyword – I Serve

Strength – Loyal, hardworking, kind, analytical

Weakness – Shy, over-worked, access people too much, unnecessarily worried

Virgo is the sixth sign of the zodiac and ruled by Mercury. This sign is known for dedicating all its time and effort on serving other people. Virgo has a knack for taking care of things around like no other. They are highly analytical and believe in perfection. They take cleanliness and hygiene way too seriously. People born under this sign have a tendency to over analyze themselves and others too.

Virgo is represented by the symbol Virgin, which makes this sign modest and very close to humanity. Their practical and logical side makes them extremely great with fact-findings and digging deep when it comes to an analytical task.

Virgos are filled with energy and drive which makes them great at their jobs as well as an enthusiastic social partner. Whether at work, home or social gathering, Virgos pay attention to detail when analyzing a situation. They are also known to criticize themselves to better their own performance. You can call it their way of self-motivation.

Virgos can be picky about what they want in their lives and homes which includes both material and people. They can never get tired of material possessions in their lives. Being perfectionist means that they like taking care of themselves too. Don't be surprised if you see a Virgo being incessantly worried about their health and diet because it comes quite naturally to a Virgo. They believe in looking good, owning good things and being in a clean place.

Virgos aren't very close to their family but they'll be around for close ones when it counts. They are ready to lend a helping hand to a friend when needed.

Compatibility: Virgos are most compatible with Cancer, Taurus, Capricorn, Scorpio and Pisces. When it comes to love, Virgos don't often take initiatives and wait for their partners to do so. This is just their way of concealing their need for love. They also don't express or talk about their true feelings but aren't afraid to show it either. Just like every other thing in their life Virgos always look for perfection in a life partner.

7. Libra

Libra (September 24 – October 23)
Symbol – The Scales

Element – Air
Compatibility – Aquarius, Leo, Capricorn, Gemini, Virgo, Libra, Sagittarius
Conflicting Signs – Cancer, Aries, Taurus, Pisces
Key Attributes – Social, artistic, indecisive, talkative, and intellectual
Strength – Social, cooperative, gracious, neutral opinions
Weakness – Indecisive, resentful, fear of confrontation
Ruling Planet – Venus
Keyword – I balance

Libra is the seventh sign of the zodiac and ruled by Venus. Libra is an intelligent sign with an ability to lead a group. This sign loves to socialize and being around people all the time, so much that they loathe the thought of being alone. Librans can take lead of everything, be it a conversation, work task or a party.

Their quick thinking makes them great at getting work done efficiently.

People born under this sign are brilliant at communicating and can hold a conversation for hours in any situation. Their quality of communication makes them great friends, co-workers and even mediators.

Their number one priority is to be liked by everyone, even if it means going the extra mile to please people. Libras try to make everyone around them feel safe and comfortable which allows other people to share their feelings with ease.

This sign takes impartial decisions and mostly have neutral opinions about situations just like its symbol *'the scale'*. They have high moral values and are never unfair with people. But there is another reason why Libras are fair and even-handed. It's because they would do anything to avoid confrontation. They dislike conflicts as they appreciate and try to create a balanced, harmonious environment around them.

Libra is rules by Venus, a smooth seductress. This means Libras are naturally charming in their own ways. Their delightful conversation style can instantly appeal anyone. Libras don't hold back when it comes to talking and have an uncanny quality to make the other person comfortable.

Compatibility: Librans are compatible with Aquarius, Leo, Capricorn, Gemini, Virgo, Libra and Sagittarius. Finding a partner is an important aspect for Librans as being alone isn't their style and doesn't come naturally to them. They are affectionate, expressive and most importantly they can talk their feelings with ease. They make great partners and when married, their foremost priority is to maintain the harmony of their marriage.

8. Scorpio

Scorpio (October 24 – November 22)
Symbol – The Scorpion

Element – Water
Compatibility – Cancer, Taurus, Scorpio, Capricorn, Pisces, Virgo, Sagittarius
Conflicting Signs – Gemini, Leo, Libra, Aquarius, Aries
Key Attributes – Passionate, secretive, insensitive, stubborn, determined, and faithful
Ruling Planet – Mars & Pluto
Keyword – I will
Strength – Bright, brave, passionate, loyal, true friend
Weakness – Secretive, violent, sarcastic, jealous

Scorpio is the eighth sign of the zodiac and ruled by water. Astrologers refer to this sign as a solid water sign, as in *'ice'*. The element alone explains a lot about their behaviour. Behind that nonchalant exterior, hides an intense and mysterious interior.

These people are not big fans of talking a lot but have their own ways of making other people gage their feelings without saying anything. Once they put their mind to something, they ensure to achieve it. These folks are loyal towards everything close to them including work, relationships, family and friends. They are hard-working and make a point to create a good impression at their jobs.

Scorpions often hide their feeling to an extent that it becomes difficult to express their feelings and passion at some point. Though they talk less but when they do they can be brutally honest and sometimes perceived as insensitive. They like the mystery in life as it gives them a thrill and excitement to keep going.

A Scorpion's loyalty is one of a kind. They may not be the ones to call you everyday but if you are close enough, they will remember you for the rest of their lives. Scorpions keep their family close and like taking care of them too. They are good with chores and managing tasks.

Compatibility: Scorpions are compatible with Cancer, Taurus, Scorpio, Capricorn, Pisces, Virgo, and Sagittarius. Out of all the signs, Scorpio is probably the most passionate when it comes to romantic relationships. In the bedroom, this sign is creative and takes intimacy seriously. In a partner, Scorpio seeks trust, loyalty and unconditional love.

9. Sagittarius

Sagittarius (November 23 - December 22)
Symbol – The Centaur

Element – Fire
Compatibility – Aries, Aquarius, Leo, Libra
Conflicting Signs – Cancer, Libra, Taurus, Capricorn and Virgo
Key Attributes – Honest, generous, reckless, relaxed, and forgiving
Ruling Planet – Jupiter
Keyword – I expand
Strength – Generous, sense of humor, visionary
Weakness – Impatient, straight-forward (sometime rude), makes promises can't keep

Sagittarius is the ninth sign of the zodiac and is ruled by Jupiter. These people are inquisitive about everything in life. This makes them avid enthusiasts of exploring unusual places around the globe. People born under this sign are joyful and look at life in a positive light no matter what. One of the reasons behind it is its ruling planet Jupiter, also known as *'Jove'* which equals Sags' jolly nature.

Those born under this sign are deep thinkers and patiently retain all the information they can get to answer their own well-though questions about life. Their love for knowledge and association with Jupiter makes them both, intelligent and lucky.

Sags are full of energy and stamina which makes most of them good athlete. They are all about adventure and seek some or the other action in life. They are confident and have a great sense of humor which effortlessly attracts quality people into their lives. They are fun to be around and love socializing with new people to share their experiences with. Sags have a broad-minded approach towards life in general which makes people comfortable to share their own viewpoints on similar subjects. Their outgoing nature demands independence and space, sometimes.

Compatibility – Sags are most compatible with Aries, Aquarius, Leo and Libra. In romantic relationships Sags are the most fun and playful. They love making their partner smile all the time. They are passionate, devoted and expressive lovers. In a partner they look for similar traits and prefer an outgoing companion to explore the world with.

10. Capricorn

Capricorn (December 23 – January 20)
Symbol – The Goat

Element – Earth

Compatibility – Capricorn, Cancer, Taurus, Libra, Scorpio, Pisces, Virgo

Conflicting Signs – Leo, Gemini, Aries, Sagittarius, Aquarius

Key Attributes – Credulous, practical, loving, sympathetic, moody, over-reactive, charitable and sensual

Ruling Planet – Saturn

Keyword – I economise

Strength – Good manager, responsible, strong self-control, sense of humor, disciplined

Weakness – Pride, unforgiving, supercilious, negative thinker

Capricorn is the tenth sign of the zodiac, ruled by Saturn and its element is Earth. Capricorn is that one sign which is both hard working and cautious. And when we say hard working, imagine the heights of hard work, that's how Capricorns like to work. They are highly ambitious and have big dreams to earn a lot of money and achieve success and most Capricorns do. Those born under this sign are fairly lazy but when it comes to work, they give in their all to complete their jobs.

Capricorn-born dwell so much into work, ambition and achieving success that their life pattern becomes more business-like. They possess a leadership approach and do whatever it takes to reach the pinnacle.

They take their job/task pretty seriously and can hold grudges against other people who are not driven enough or come in the way. However, the grudge goes away when the Capricorn reaches the top. The best quality of Capricorns is their practical approach towards life. They know that things don't come easy in life, so they are willing to work hard to earn it. They stay far away from a fantasy-land and deal with life pragmatically, one day at a time.

Capricorns grow up pretty early and don't depend on anyone for help. They are very independent and have realistic goals and dreams in life. Their philosophy is to live life on their own terms and never compromise.

Compatibility: They are most compatible with Cancer, Taurus, Libra, Scorpio, Capricorn, Pisces and Virgo. As mentioned above, being cautious is one of their evident traits and that applies to their love life as well. They like to go slow and steady in a romantic relationship without jumping into something they are not ready for. They are not big on effective communication, so to understand a Capricorn you should pay attention to his/her actions.

11. Aquarius

Aquarius (January 21 – February 19)
Symbol – The Water Bearer

Element – Air
Compatibility – Aries, Sagittarius, Gemini, Libra
Conflicting Signs – Cancer, Leo, Virgo, Pisces, Scorpio, Capricorn
Key Attributes – Intellectual, sympathetic, unpredictable, confident, liberal, kind
Ruling Planet – Uranus & Saturn
Keyword – I progress
Strength – Original, independent, kind, progressive
Weakness – Aloof, inflexible, over-emotional

Aquarius is the eleventh sign of the zodiac and is ruled by Uranus and Saturn. These folks are readily available to take on humanitarian tasks and genuinely wish for the world to be a better place. Aquarians are always surrounded by like-minded people and are quick to share their own ideas about improving the world.

Those born under this sign are bright and very creative with unique thoughts to deliver tasks. Aquarians love to share their ideas but only with the ones who genuinely respect their minds. If an Aquarian has a hunch that someone's mocking his/her thoughts and creativity he/she won't hesitate to show them what that really feel like.

Sometimes these folks may be perceived as shy but when they start talking, they can go on for hours. Aquarians don't trust people that easily. Their intellectual mind attracts many people every day but when it comes to close friends, they have just about a handful.

This sign is ruled by Saturn and Uranus. Saturn was the most powerful ancient God while Uranus was the oldest in Roman mythology. These two together generate strong energy and intelligence in a person born under this sign. They are quick and efficient to complete their tasks and always look forward to accomplish something new in life.

Compatibility: Aquarians are most compatible with four signs Aries, Sagittarius, Gemini and Libra. Being so intellectually stimulated makes them fancy people who possess the same level of intelligence to pull together a healthy conversation with these folks. They can talk on and on about anything, culture, the world, science, the galaxy (you know what I mean). In a partner they specifically look for loyalty and long term commitment.

12. Pisces

Pisces (February 20 – March 20)
Symbol – The Fish

Element – Water

Compatibility – Taurus, Cancer, Aries, Scorpio, Sagittarius, Capricorn, Pisces

Conflicting Signs – Leo, Gemini, Virgo, Libra, Aquarius

Key Attributes – Sensitive, spiritual, loving, intuitive, vulnerable, and moody

Ruling Planet – Jupiter & Neptune

Keyword – I sacrifice

Strength – Compassionate, gentle, musical, intelligent, intuitive, understanding, liberal

Weakness – Overly-trusting, over-sensitive, vulnerable

Pisces is the twelfth and last sign of the zodiac and it is ruled by Jupiter, the ancient king of Gods and Neptune the ruler of the seas. Those planets are really powerful together and result in Pisceans' influential, compassionate, sensitive and generous nature. This helps these people understand every person from every perspectives and become close with others by gaining their unconditional trust.

Those born under this sign are dreamy and sometimes find it difficult to separate reality from their dream world. They believe in all possibilities and that everything is doable if they put their mind to it.

These folks have a strong persona to impress people around them even when they don't express much through words. This sign is a creative and artistic lot with passion for music and nature. Their compassionate and loving nature also makes them very generous towards their loved ones. They are not very great with managing their life and time effectively which makes them juggle life and tying to make everyone happy. They are quick-witted and fun to be around.

Compatibility: Being a water sign, Pisces is attracted to fellow water signs like Cancer and Scorpio. Also, Aries, Sagittarius and Capricorn. They are passionate and would do anything for their loved ones, as per their keyword *'I sacrifice'*. When it comes to love, they are hardcore romantics, the old school kind who love bringing gifts and flowers even on a normal day. They are loyal and don't care for short term relationships. In a partner they look for intimate, deep connection and reciprocation of compassion and affection.

Final Words

Note that the dates may be differ on all sources. This discrepancy is caused by leap year and also because the sun does not move in the same speed every year which may affect the dates of these signs. These characterizations were rather brief but hope they gave you a fair idea of individual signs and their traits.

Thank You Page

I want to personally thank you for reading my book. I hope you found information in this book useful and I would be very grateful if you could leave your honest review about this book. I certainly want to thank you in advance for doing this.

If you have the time, you can check my other books too.

www.ingramcontent.com/pod-product-compliance
Lightning Source LLC
LaVergne TN
LVHW021742060526
838200LV00052B/3425